*The Reverend Augustus Orlebar in the
Vicarage garden at Willington c.1910*

THE REVEREND AUGUSTUS ORLEBAR

'Squarson', sportsman and 'Father of the Village'
Vicar of Willington 1858-1912

* * * * *

Gordon Vowles

The Gostwick Press (Willington)

First Published 2010
by
The Gostwick Press (Willington)
in association with Willington Local History Group
and
the Friends of Willington Parish Church

ISBN: 978-0-9565663-0-0

Typeset, designed and printed by Creamers of Luton

Front and back cover:
Parish Church of St. Lawrence, Willington viewed from the north-west
and the Reverend Augustus Orlebar in later life.

CONTENTS

LIST OF ILLUSTRATIONS

SOURCES OF ILLUSTRATIONS

The majority of the illustrations are reproduced from originals or copies held by the Beds. and Luton Archives and Records Service (The frontispiece and cover and Nos. 4, 5, 6, 8, 9, 10, 11, 12, 13, 14, 15, 16 and 17.)   No. 1 is reproduced by kind permission of Richard West and other Trustees of the Bernard West Estate.   Nos. 2 and 3 are taken from Macmillan's 1869 edition of *Tom Brown's School Days* and Nos. 7 and 18 are from photographs by Bryan Buckby.

PREFACE AND ACKNOWLEDGEMENTS

This brief appreciation of the life of the Rev. Augustus Orlebar arises out of a talk given to members of the Willington Local History Group (W.L.H.G.) in March 2009. In preparing for that talk, I came to have a high regard for this Victorian clergyman who dedicated his life for over half a century to the spiritual and social welfare of the villagers of Willington. As a Trustee of the Friends of Willington Parish Church I decided to turn my researches into a modest monograph as a tribute to this remarkable man and, through its sale, make a contribution to the funds of the Friends for the maintenance of the fabric of the Church which meant so much to him.

Although none of Augustus's writings in the form of diaries or sermons have come down to us, there are some useful records, including 'scrapbooks' of newspaper cuttings and family papers, compiled by members of the Orlebar family. In addition, there are 'official' records such as School logbooks, School Board minutes and Vestry minutes. All these documents are lodged with the Bedfordshire & Luton Archives & Records Service (BLARS) whose staff, as always, have been extremely helpful in drawing my attention to them. Sheila Ward, Archivist of W.L.H.G., also kindly spent time digging out from the Group's archives information on the village in the 19th century which also proved very useful. I have also included a select bibliography of secondary sources which I have also consulted.

Early drafts of the text were read and commented on by Rob Bollington, Bryan Buckby, James Collett-White, Dorothy Jamieson and Sheila Ward and I am grateful to them all for the trouble they took in doing this and for the constructive comments they made. In addition, without Rob Bollington's and Bryan Buckby's help I would never have been able to get the text and illustrations in a form acceptable to the Printer for publication. I am most grateful to them both for their patience and forbearance in supporting a far from proficient computer operator.

Gordon Vowles
Willington, May 2010

The Reverend Augustus Orlebar

Victorian Country Clergyman

Introduction and Early Years

The Rev. Augustus Orlebar, member of a long established and distinguished Bedfordshire family, is typical of many Victorian country clergymen. Educated and with wide interests and accomplishments, they not only administered to the spiritual needs of their parishioners - and invariably repaired and restored their churches as well - but also took a lead in seeking to improve, as part of their pastoral duties, the welfare of the village communities nominally placed within their care. At a time when the responsibilities and actions of the State were many fewer than they are today and the countryside was subject to the impact of ever accelerating change, there was ample opportunity for a parson with a social conscience to initiate developments for the betterment of his 'flock' in fulfilment of the Victorian Church of England's sense of mission to the poor. In no area was this of greater significance than in village education. It was also not unusual for a Victorian country parson to spend the greater part of his working life in the same parish, although fifty-four years - the length of Orlebar's incumbency at Willington - was exceptional. These long tenures meant parsons came to know their village communities well and, because of commitment to the well-being of their parishioners, they became much revered and respected local figures. Such a parson was the Rev. Augustus Orlebar.

Augustus Orlebar, born in 1824, was the seventh son and youngest of the ten children of Robert Charles Orlebar and spent his early years in the family home at Crawley House, near Aspley Guise, in Bedfordshire. His father was a member of a collateral branch of the Orlebar family which had Northamptonshire origins, deriving its name from the village of Orlingbury. In the mid-16th century they migrated to Bedfordshire, holding land in the north of the County in the parishes of Harrold, Pavenham and Podington and were granted a coat of arms in 1662. As members of the landed gentry they made a significant contribution to the life and affairs of both their native and adopted counties throughout the 17th and 18th centuries as justices of the peace, high sheriffs and members of Parliament; many were lawyers and Augustus's great grandfather, John, was one of the M.P.s for the Borough of Bedford from 1727 until 1734. As a result of a judicious marriage settlement, in the early 18th century Richard Orlebar was able to build, probably acting in part as his own architect, a fine, small stone country seat, Hinwick House, in the parish of Podington.

When Augustus was born, George IV, better known as the Prince Regent, was king and Queen Victoria would not ascend the throne until little more than a decade later in 1837. The England of 1824 was still recovering from the long war against the French and Napoleon and government, power and influence were still firmly vested in the hands of the rich and propertied classes. But the country was on the verge of colossal change in social attitudes and technological development: England was about to become the leading industrial world power – 'the workshop of the world' – with territorial possessions spread across the globe and constituting the greatest imperial power ever known. The Britain which Augustus left in 1912 was indeed very different from the country into which he had been born nearly ninety years earlier. It had changed from a predominantly respectful rural society into a land in which the majority of the population were less deferential town dwellers. The coming of railways had long transformed the nation. The State was increasingly assuming responsibility for people's lives and the First World War was about to change the country forever. Yet Augustus's Willington – of the church and the rural countryside – whilst by no means immune from the impact of all these changes, was less affected by their pace and intensity so that the traditional values of service and concern for others remained more alive there than in many places elsewhere.

We know nothing of Augustus's very early years, although it is likely that initially he was educated at home.   In 1836 he attended at Podington the funeral of his great uncle and head of the family, John Richard Orlebar.   The next year brought death - an all too frequent visitor in the early 19th century - even nearer to home when his father, Robert Charles, and his mother, Charlotte, both died.   Orphaned he was adopted by his uncle and godfather, William Augustus Orlebar, and went to live with him at Hinwick Hall, a house dating from the 16th century and adjacent to Hinwick House.   In 1838 he was confirmed at Sharnbrook, collected money for Queen Victoria's coronation festivities and is recorded as saying Latin lessons to his uncle in preparation, no doubt, for the commencement of his formal education at school.

1. Hinwick Hall from a drawing by Bemard West.

Education and Training

The school chosen by his uncle was Rugby, then, as now, one of the leading public boarding schools. William Augustus took his nephew himself to the School, recording in his diary: 'Left Augustus, poor boy, at Dr. Arnold's, at Rugby School: God prosper the undertaking.' Was Augustus, it has to be wondered, already displaying an independence of spirit and strength of character which he was to show in large measure in adult life?

Dr. Thomas Arnold is considered by many to be the doyen of Victorian public school clergyman headmasters: at Rugby he broadened the curriculum, improved discipline, made the chapel the centre of school life and contributed greatly to an improvement in the image of these schools in the eyes of the professional and ruling classes. But there may have been a more personal reason why Augustus was despatched to Rugby and not a boarding school elsewhere. Arnold's wife Mary was a member of the Penrose family and the Orlebars and Penroses were related by marriage. Mrs. Arnold's nephew, John Penrose, spent sometime as a curate at Podington.

There is no record of Augustus's academic performance whilst at Rugby where he remained until 1842, the year of Dr. Arnold's death. However, we know much more about his developing sporting prowess which he continued to display throughout later life. At Rugby under Arnold games became a means of character building and were not seen as mere healthy exercise or a means of keeping youthful exuberance in check. Augustus found his way into the School cricket 1st XI, although he does not appear to have particularly distinguished himself with either bat or ball. His forte was in the field and in 1841 in a match against the M.C.C. he pulled off a stunning catch at cover point to dispose of the opposition's best batsmen, resulting in a victory for the School team. He succeeded to the captaincy of the School XI in 1842. Arnold refined the prefect system at

Rugby and, as a sporty senior pupil, Augustus must have joined its ranks. Arnold, also an important figure in the Church, sought to turn out 'muscular Christian young men', fulfilled, self-confident, imbued with a moral earnestness and ready to serve their fellow men – and women – in a variety of honourable human endeavours.   In 1911, reminiscing in an interview with a *Daily Mail* reporter, Augustus recalled his schooldays of 'icy-cold baths' on winter mornings 'lit by a pale match held aloft'.   He went on, not unusually when the old look at the conduct of younger generations, to condemn 1911 youths as being 'soft, pampered and coddled'.

2. *'Cricket match' from Macmillan's 1869 edition of
Tom Brown's School Days by Thomas Hughes.*

This interest by a national newspaper in Augustus's schooldays some seventy years on was because he had featured in what was probably the most popular Victorian novel on public school life, *Tom Brown's School Days* by Thomas Hughes, a contemporary at Rugby. In 1911 Hughes was long dead and Augustus was almost the last surviving 'boy' who had knowledge of the incidents on which Hughes based events in the novel. There were claims that the hero, Tom Brown, was Augustus, whilst there were other assertions, perhaps even more implausible, that Hughes took the character of Arthur, a diligent student and top of his form, from Augustus. The octagenarian interviewee did nothing to clarify these assertions and nor could he possibly have ever done so. The truth is most likely that Hughes drew characters in the book which were a blend of his various schoolboy companions. What, however, is absolutely certain is that one of the most dramatic incidents in the novel – the fight between Tom Brown and Slogger Williams and 'one of the most striking bouts of fisticuffs in English fiction' – was based on an actual event involving Augustus in which in the novel he assumed the role of Tom. Augustus recalled clearly in his old age that the fight took place, when both contestants were aged seventeen, on a wet day in 1841 in the School House hall and not in the close behind the chapel as Hughes described. What sparked the fight was an impulsive act on the part of Augustus: passing through the hall carrying a fives bat he came across Slogger Williams (real name, Bulkeley Jones) leaning forward over a low wall reading and displaying an inviting and bulky posterior. The temptation to give him a whack with the bat was too great for Augustus to resist. Jones was rightly incensed by the unprovoked attack and a determined and bloody encounter between the two ensued. When a noisy crowd of boys gathered to witness the contest, the combatants were only parted when Dr. Arnold appeared, shocked that senior pupils were engaged in such a furious fracas and dispensed to both contestants two hundred lines of Virgil to learn as punishment for their unseemly conduct. Subsequently, in a true spirit of Christian reconciliation, Augustus and Jones became lifelong friends and correspondents. Jones became Chancellor of the Diocese of St. Asaph in North Wales.

From Rugby Augustus progressed to Wadham College, Oxford, matriculating in May 1843. This was a natural enough progression at the time. The ancient universities of Oxford and Cambridge were still only

3. 'The Fight' from Macmillan's 1869 edition of
Tom Brown's School Days by Thomas Hughes.

open to the sons of the rich and privileged members of the Church of England. Religious tests which excluded Roman Catholic and Protestant Nonconformists were not abolished until the mid-1850s and then only for first degrees. Like so much else in Victorian society, the universities were in need of reform. There was little study for research and they had become an unsatisfactory means of education for clergymen, lawyers, doctors and landed gentlemen. Again, as at Rugby, we know more of Augustus's sporting achievements at Oxford than his academic studies. He played cricket for the University but he did not gain a 'blue' since he did not play in any games against Cambridge. At home in 1844 he taught his cousin, Richard, to skate and swim.

Nor do we know when and how Augustus decided to enter the Church. The priesthood was seen by many younger sons as a fitting occupation after university for a gentleman who did not have an inclination to become a lawyer or a soldier, both careers requiring further financial outlay. (The purchase of commissions in the army was not abolished until 1871.) In addition, priestly duties were unlikely to be too onerous and ample time could therefore be spent in scholarly and sporting pursuits. Whilst personal conviction and a sense of vocation may not have been paramount, the priesthood offered the opportunity of a life of service to others in a secure setting. Even if Augustus had decided to enter the Church when he 'went up' to Oxford, a degree course in theology was not offered there until 1870 so that he 'read' classics, in which he had been schooled at Rugby. He graduated in 1847 and took his M.A. in 1850. Like all ordinands of his day, Augustus would have had to satisfy the bishop on his status, moral character and intellectual abilities, in all probability as a result of a cursory oral examination conducted by the bishop's examining chaplain. Provided he had a job to go to, usually a curacy, the ordinand was then considered ready to commence his duties.

Years as a Curate

Augustus received no training in a theological college, as would be the case today, since such colleges were few and far between. (Eight theological colleges were founded between 1836 and 1876, although residential training for ordinands did not become compulsory until 1909.) Such professional training for clergy as there was at the time was, therefore, mainly 'on the job' as a curate in a parish, provided that the vicar or rector was present in the parish to offer supervision and undertake a mentoring role. Augustus was ordained deacon in 1847 by the Bishop of Chichester and served for two years as curate in the parishes of Southover and All Saints, Lewes, in Sussex, becoming a priest in 1848. Augustus's mentor was the Rev. John Scobell, who, as a non-resident honorary canon or prebendary of the cathedral in Chichester and the holder of two livings, certainly required the services of a curate. Even after the passage of the Pluralities Act in 1838, which largely abolished the holding of more than one living, clergymen were still permitted to do so provided the total population of the two parishes was less than three thousand, the distance between the two churches was not more than ten miles and the joint annual income from the livings was under £1000. What salary a curate received was a matter between him and his vicar or rector. Augustus, therefore, found himself pitched into a busy round of parish duties without any form of professional training. This was the usual practice throughout most of the 19th century, the junior ranks of the clergy being filled, in the main, by poorly paid, university educated, gentlemanly amateurs. In his short stay in Sussex, Augustus was not so overworked, however, that he failed to notice that his employer had an attractive and talented daughter, of which more anon.

Good training is to be gained from a variety of experiences. From 1850 to 1852 Augustus served as curate to Lord Lyttelton's brother 'Billy' (Rev. the Hon. William Henry Lyttelton) at the estate church of Hagley Hall in Worcestershire. His duties there were in all probability very different from those which he had undertaken in Lewes. The spiritual and pastoral needs of the estate workers would have occupied only some of his time. It is likely, too, that he had some contact and duties with the Lyttelton household at the Hall. The Lytteltons were a very religious family of a High Church persuasion with which Augustus may not have been altogether comfortable. George, 4th Baron Lyttelton, by his first wife, who was the sister-in-law of the future prime minister William Gladstone, eventually had a brood of twelve children, of whom eight were boys. It was later claimed that Augustus had taught the Lyttelton children to play cricket and he may, indeed, have been responsible for introducing the game to a family which became obsessed with it. George Lyttelton, a manic depressive, had succeeded to the title and the Hagley estate in 1837 and certainly, whilst the older children were very young, there is no evidence of a family obsession with cricket. Later, however, a cricket pitch was set up immediately outside the drawing room window of the Hall and the long gallery was put to cricketing use when the weather was inclement.   The girls were required by their brothers to chase and pick up balls and stand for hours at long-stop. The highlight of the Hagley sporting year became the annual family cricket match against Bromsgrove Boys' School. All the Lyttelton boys, except one, in turn found their way into the Eton XI, whilst Alfred, the youngest who was not born until 1857, was a multiple 'blue' at Cambridge and in the 1880s not only played soccer and cricket for England but was also the best lawn tennis player of his time. Was it, then, Augustus who sparked all this off? At any rate, because of his association with the family and his own athletic prowess, Augustus must have followed these later Lyttelton sporting achievements at least with interest if not with feelings of some personal satisfaction and credit. Certainly, his family scrapbook of press cuttings includes a number of reports of events in April 1876 when the fifty-nine year old George Lyttelton, in a dark fit of melancholia, threw himself over the banisters of the staircase of his London house, dying a day later of a broken pelvis and a shock induced heart attack.

Return to Bedfordshire and coming to Willington

After Augustus returned to his native county in 1852, he continued to play cricket with the Tylecote family at Marston Moretaine and he also turned out for the XXIIs of Bedfordshire, Northamptonshire and Uppingham in matches against All England. His return to the County resulted from being offered the living of Farndish, located in the north of the County in close proximity to Hinwick and Podington and then a small parish of only 82 souls and 15 inhabited houses. He remained there until January 1858. There was no parsonage in the parish and he lived either with his sister, Emily, in Wellingborough or with his godfather at Hinwick Hall, riding over to Farndish on horseback. It is unlikely that he found his parish duties arduous which enabled him to pursue his sporting activities and country pursuits without feelings of guilty neglect. On Sunday the minimum requirement for public worship was the reading of Mattins and Evensong with the evening service, particularly during the winter months, often conducted during the afternoon. These services were dominated by the sermon and the saying, not singing, of the responses and the psalms, although often inaudibly. The interval between the two services might be filled with the performance of baptisms, marriages, burials and churchings. As the 19th century progressed Holy Communion became more frequent, with a move from quarterly to monthly celebrations becoming the norm. Daily Offices were usually not observed on the part of priests. However, there is no evidence that Augustus shirked his parish duties when compared with the generally accepted practices of the time. In 1857 he gave a paten to the Church, possibly a leaving present. In 1859 a successor at Farndish, the Rev. Samuel Lyon, noted that the church services were well attended which may have been a legacy of Augustus's endeavours in the parish.

In 1858 Augustus was offered the living of Willington by Francis, 8th Duke of Bedford, the village being part of the Russell estates. (The 4th Duke had purchased the manor of Willington from the Duke of

Marlborough in 1774.) The living in 1858 had an annual value of £230 at the time whereas at Farndish it had been only £140. (Derived from the ancient system of tithes - theoretically a tenth part of a person's income - they were the main source of a priest's maintenance. A rector, not always a priest, received the great tithes and a vicar the small tithes. Originally paid in kind, in 1836 tithes were replaced with a rent charge on land.) When commutation was applied to Willington in 1840 the parish had a total acreage of 1648 which included 201 acres of woodland and 19 acres of glebe, the latter assigned to the priest which he was able to work as a further source of income. Even so, Willington was still only a small village with a population of 282 at the time of the 1851 census and half a dozen or

3. The Vicarage, Church Road, Willington, in the early 20th century showing extension to the rear before demolition.

so tenant farmers, the biggest being William Brimley at Road or Grange Farm of 382 acres; Hill or Lane Farm was of 298 acres, Croot's Farm 247 acres and Manor or Park Farm 226 acres. Augustus's predecessor as vicar had been the Rev. Henry Fuller who had been presented to the living in 1834. On his arrival, Fuller had a farmhouse on the north side of Church Road converted into a vicarage and the glebe land, previously dispersed in the open fields, consolidated around the vicarage and including a dovecote. However, it is recorded in 1847 that Fuller was non-resident. Augustus, on the other hand, had the need to prepare the vicarage for becoming a family home. His godfather, William Augustus, carried out an inspection of the vicarage in 1858, perhaps prior to helping his nephew financially to put the house into good order.

1858 was an eventful year for Augustus since he not only commenced his fifty-four year tenure of office as vicar of Willington, but it was also the year in which he became engaged to Caroline Yarde Scobell, the daughter of the Rev. John Scobell, the rector under whom he had 'trained' in Lewes between 1847 and 1849. Caroline was thirty years old, four years younger than her husband-to-be. There is, however, no reference to what might have been a lengthy courtship. The couple were married in 1859 by the Bishop of Chichester in the Cathedral and the groom brought his bride to the vicarage at Willington which remained their family home together until Caroline died in March 1904. They were to bring up six children there, four sons and two daughters: Augustus, born 1860; Caroline, 1862; Evelyn, 1863; George, 1866; Margaret, 1870 and Edward, 1872 – the two eldest named respectively after their father and mother.

Early Years as Vicar of Willington

There was a need for Augustus to provide financially for this growing family and maintain them in a life style appropriate to their social standing and Augustus's position as scholar, religious leader and 'top man' of the village community. With the Duke of Bedford the sole but absent landlord, Augustus was, in effect, both parson and substitute squire. He was what has been termed 'a squarson' with no one above him in the social order of those resident in the village. In addition, he was the sole person of education in the community.

The income from the parish living, plus 'surplice fees' from baptisms, weddings and funerals, was far from adequate to keep the family in the style which they and others therefore expected   Only a small number of domestic staff were employed at the vicarage, as the census returns show: a cook, a housemaid and, when the children were young, a nursemaid and later a needlewoman.   Outside the house, the vicarage garden, the working of the glebe and attention to horses and other livestock required one or two further male staff, either engaged on a permanent or casual basis.   As the family grew in size, more accommodation was needed in the vicarage and alterations and additions were made in 1868, undertaken by the Bedford surveyor, Alfred Adams, and perhaps paid for by Augustus's godfather.   Census returns record a vicarage of twelve rooms, excluding sculleries, landings, lobbies, closets and bathrooms. As they became older, the boys, but not the girls, were boarders at leading public schools – Eton, Marlborough and Radley - and three of the boys then went on to 'Oxbridge', all, of course, at not inconsiderable expense.   There is no evidence that Augustus inherited any wealth, although this might well have been the case. As the youngest son, it was very unlikely that he received anything following the death of his father, although his uncle and godfather, William Augustus, who adopted him, died in 1873, had no children and a reputation for generosity: Augustus referred to him in 1864 as 'one of those ready givers, too ready sometimes'. There is every evidence to show that William Augustus was a good godfather to Augustus so he had every reason for making this statement. The Orlebars were a prolific family – Augustus's father was one of twelve – so that bequests could have come from any number of uncles and aunts and other relations, although unlikely. When William Augustus's wife, Mary, died in 1859, he was given her 'dear old pony carriage'.

5. Augustus and Caroline Orlebar c.1860.

However, these would have been irregular and uncertain means of income and Augustus needed to supplement his earnings from more regular and reliable sources. He decided to exploit his own educational background by tutoring young men of good family in preparation for them 'going up' to university. This was something which could be undertaken in his own home without getting in the way of his duties as parish priest. As early as 1860 when visiting his uncle and godfather, William Augustus, at Hinwick Hall, he was accompanied by his pupil the young baronet, Sir Bruce Chichester (1842-81), who is also recorded as being resident at Willington vicarage in the census return of the following year. Chichester had inherited the title and his father's estate, Arlington Court in north Devon, in 1851; he had been educated at Harrow but did not proceed to university, so that he may have proved an unreceptive pupil. (It may have been that Augustus's father-in-law, the Rev. John Scobell, was instrumental in introducing Chichester to Augustus since he was also a member of an old Devon family.) There are more details in the mid-1870s of the tutoring of Sir Philip Payne (1858-1935) of Wootton, prior to his progressing to Magdalen College, Cambridge. Payne had inherited the baronetcy and his estate at the age of 15. He was resident with the Orlebars in Willington from 1874-7 and invoices for that period exist for tuition and board, the going rate for an academic term being about £100. At Christmas 1874 Sir Philip was also charged 'extras' of nine guineas for the boarding of a groom and a pony, £2 5s. for dogs and £1 10s. for laundry. This additional income was undoubtedly welcome, and clearly profitable, but how frequent and continuous it was is uncertain.

Later, in the 1880s, a press advertisement shows that Augustus wished to let the Vicarage – 'near river' - for a period of six weeks during the summer at a weekly rate of eight guineas or ten guineas with servants, horse and carriage, boat and garden produce. If taken up, the income would have helped to meet the cost of the family decamping elsewhere on holiday. Whatever the total size of Augustus's income and from whatever number of different sources it came, it is clear that the family were able to enjoy a comfortable life style, mixing socially on equal terms with the 'best' families in the locality.   On his death in 1912 Augustus's will was proved in the not inconsiderable sum for the time of £19,545 gross, £16,829 net.

It is unfortunate that no diaries which Augustus may have kept have survived.   Nor are there records of the enormous number of sermons which he must have delivered during his lengthy incumbency and which would have given clues to his personal faith and Christian beliefs.   The 19th century was a time of revolution and revival for the Church of England and its life was marked by tensions, controversies and wide differences, as it is to this day.   It was not a unified body; there were distinct 'parties' displaying different attitudes not only to liturgical and ceremonial practices but also on matters of doctrine and belief.   At one end of the spectrum were the 'Low Church' Evangelicals who stressed the authority of the Bible with personal emphasis on devotion and piety.   At the other end were the 'High Church' Tractarians who emphasised the Catholic and apostolic character of the established church with emphasis upon ritual and ceremony.   In the middle were the followers of a more liberal 'Broad Church' with commitment to tolerance of a breadth of theological opinions but concerned that Christianity should be made active in the lives of individuals.

It is only possible to speculate where Augustus stood in this wide spectrum of views and beliefs.   In attempting an assessment of his character and personality, he does not appear to have been drawn to extremes.   On so many issues he seems to have adopted a balanced, level-headed and pragmatic approach.   He was a man of wide interests unlikely to be attracted to narrow and limiting philosophies.   Certainly, Augustus gives no evidence of an unseemly exhibition of religious zeal.   Publicly, he made no reference to the challenge of science to belief or the reconciliation of faith and reason.   When it came to restoring the parish church of St. Lawrence at Willington, it was undertaken in a restrained fashion without any of the trappings of Catholic forms of ritual and ceremony. Moreover, Dr. Thomas Arnold, undoubtedly an important influence on Augustus, loathed both Tractarians and 'Low' churchmen in equal measure. He urged a broader, more critical and less dogmatic approach to theology. The parish of Willington had been transferred from the diocese of Lincoln to that of Ely in 1837 - and no further change took place until 1914 when it passed to the newer diocese of St. Albans. Ely, embracing as it did 'Low Church' Cambridge, was far from a 'hotbed' of 'High Church' support, unlike Oxford which was the 'birthplace' and focal point of Tractarianism. All this points to Augustus, despite himself being an Oxford man, being sympathetic to the 'Broad Church' stance. In addition, there was a Methodist chapel in the village, and pragmatist that he was, he was unlikely to have adopted and pursued views and practices which could have caused upset to villagers who otherwise might well have been prepared, turn and turn about, to have attended services at either church or chapel. Such 'itinerants' were colloquially known as 'devil dodgers', having a foot in each of the competing religious camps. Certainly, Augustus does not appear to have spent time in engaging in theological controversy; rather he put his energies into visiting parishioners in their homes, organising parish life and exercising his ministry as the arbiter of conventional morality throughout the whole village community.

Restoration of the Parish Church

Viewed from outside when Augustus became vicar in 1858, the parish church of St. Lawrence would have been much as we see it today. Thomas Fisher's engraving of 1812 of a view from the south-east shows little change over the last two hundred years. The Church is a fine specimen of late Perpendicular architecture, built in the 1530s and replacing earlier church buildings, and constructed of ashlar blocks. The Church, consisting of a nave, chancel, north aisle with a three windowed clerestory and north chapel of slightly later date than the rest, stands solid and firm with a well proportioned tower and south porch, strongly buttressed walls, large windows – particularly at the east end – and crenellated roofs. It is, however, inside in the nave, chancel and north aisle that the greatest change is to be detected.

6. South-east view of Willington Parish Church from an engraving by Thomas Fisher of 1812.

There is a description of the interior of the Church in 1847 by 'W.A.' (John Martin, Librarian to the Duke of Bedford at Woburn Abbey from 1836 to 1855), one of a series of articles on Bedfordshire churches which appeared initially in the *Northampton Mercury*. Little would have altered between then and Augustus's arrival in the parish ten years later. Martin noted that the gate to the churchyard was locked and its occupants, other than the already departed, were a cow and a calf since it was let to a local farmer for grazing. Inside the Church he went on to deplore the heavy overlay of whitewash, including the monuments and the piers of the arcading between the nave and the north aisle, which was in a 'mournful condition'. The west window in the tower had been blocked up in 1835 and a gallery formed for the choir and musicians. He applauded the absence of an organ. The nave was fitted up with open seats, i.e. not boxed, but the pulpit and reading desk were 'very poor'. The chancel, the province of the patron, the Duke of Bedford, had recently been repaired but the roof had been lowered so as to interfere with the line of the east window above the altar. The chancel was also cluttered with two large (boxed?) pews, 'resembling cages', and in a corner were a mop, scrubbing brush and dirty mats which no self-respecting churchwarden would allow in a position of prominence in his own home. There was a miserable substitute for the original font. Here was a fine church calling out for attention which Martin felt could be restored at relatively little cost. It should also be noted that earlier the wooden screen and rood loft between the chancel and the nave had been desecrated to admit the box pews mentioned above. (Ugly canopies resulted in the tracery of the screen having to be cut away.) The screen and loft were still there in damaged form in the late 1820s and removed before 1847 for repair but sadly never returned, although a press report in 1875 speaks – two years before the major restoration referred to below - of a rood loft in apparently good order!

It took Augustus a little time to initiate action on the fabric of the Church and redress the years of neglect. His first priority was to get to know his 'flock' and their needs; he had to adjust to the responsibilities of being a husband and father after a decade or more of bachelorhood; and, above all, restoration work on the Church required the getting together of funds to finance it from sources outside the parish. As the Churchwardens' records show, to begin with, therefore, improvements were small and cosmetic: already in 1856 some minor repairs had been undertaken; in 1857 fifty new hymn books were purchased for £2 10s.; and in 1860 a new cushion and lining for the pulpit and a harmonium were introduced. (Previously there was an 'orchestra' of three instruments only, violin, clarinet and bass viol.) Caroline, Augustus's wife, was musical so there was a ready accompanist, and later when the harmonium was replaced by an organ, she became organist and choirmaster. It was not until 1867 that more major improvement work was undertaken at a cost £182 which was borne nominally by William, 8th Duke of Bedford, although the Russell estates were administered by his cousin and successor as 9th Duke in 1872, Hastings Russell. The work entailed alterations to the pulpit, desk and pews, stone cleaning, filling of five windows with grisaille glass by Powell of Whitefriars and provision of the present stone font which was made by S. Jarvis of Bedford. It was recorded at the time that these improvements took place as a result of the 'untiring exertions' of Augustus, the liberality of the Duke of Bedford and the help of parishioners.

It was another ten years before the most extensive work of restoration on the Church during Augustus's incumbency was undertaken. Much earlier, soon after his arrival in Willington and cognisant of the neglected and dilapidated condition of the Church, Augustus had approached the Duke for help only to be told that Willington must wait its turn; there were many other estate parishes in the queue for ducal favour and patronage.   Eventually, the 9th Duke's promise to come up with £2500 for a major restoration enabled work to commence in 1877.   The architect for the work was Henry Clutton, prominent in London, who undertook extensive work for the Duke on his estates.   Clutton's crowning glory for the 8th Duke had been the new parish church of St. Mary in Park Street, Woburn, complete with a crypt, and built in 1865-8 at a cost of £35,000. He also designed other churches for the Duke in the County at Souldrop, Steppingley and Woburn Sands and, in addition to Willington, carried out restoration work on churches at Houghton Regis and Stevington.   (Clutton was also the architect of Willington School.)   Since he was contributing the bulk of the money, it was only natural that much of the work should have been done on the chancel, for which the Duke had a special responsibility as patron of the living.   General work included new lead on the roof, the floor levelled and made good, the taking down of the gallery at the west end and the creation of a bell chamber, the placing of heavy louvres in the belfry windows (now removed) and many pews replaced.   In the chancel, encaustic tiles were placed in the sanctuary which are said to be by Minton and copies of the original 14th century tiles found in the Church at the time of the restoration; the altar rails by Jones and Willis were set up; and the pulpit, reading desk and seats renewed in carved work.   The contractor for the work was the large London based speculative builder, William Cubbitt, and the clerk of works, William Wright.   Whilst the work was in progress, services were held in the new school.

Over and above this major restoration, Augustus was also responsible for overseeing other improvements in the Church.   Prior to the work mentioned above, in 1875 Augustus took the opportunity of purchasing an organ from Cople at a cost of £400 to replace the existing harmonium.   The organ had been built in 1857 by the Vicar of Cople, the Rev. Henry Havergal, a member of a notable musical family, composer and

conductor of the Bedford Harmonic Society, and referred to in the
Bedfordshire Times as 'an amateur production'. It must have remained in
Havergal's possession since, when he died, his executors put it up for sale.
Augustus opened a subscription list for its purchase. The Duke of Bedford
gave £100 and the tenant farmers also gave generous amounts so that the
organ was eventually transferred to Willington. The organ was
reconstructed by Messrs. Hill of London and 'made practically a new
instrument'. (It had to be repaired in 1890 – at the expense of the Duke of
Bedford – and again restored in 1925 before being replaced in 1969.) In
September 1875 a celebratory service of thanksgiving for its installation
took place with Caroline at the keyboard, stops and pedals, although a
press report stated 'some of the reeds seemed out of tune.' Caroline had
also painted a figure on the organ case. Two hundred additional chairs
were placed 'in the aisles and every corner', although still few villagers
were present. Twenty-eight robed clergy from neighbouring parishes
attended, together with the Archdeacon of Bedford and the Bishop of Ely,
the latter contributing a half hour sermon. The service concluded at 5.30
p.m. with the singing of the hymn, *Now thank we all our God* and the
offertory amounted to £28 3s. 3½d. The company retired to the vicarage
garden where a marquee had been erected on the lawn and an al fresco tea
was taken. Later, Augustus and Caroline entertained the Bishop, together
with 'a select party', to a sumptuous dinner. Quite a day!

Ever conscious of the welfare of his parishioners and particularly
those who attended services in the Church, Augustus was instrumental in
trying to heat what otherwise would have been a cold and forbidding
building - and not just on dank and dark winter days. In 1867 a stove was
installed in the Church at a cost of £60 and this in all probability is the
Gurney stove which is still in the Church, although long out of use.
Patented in 1856, over the next decade or so warm air Gurney stoves

became the main means of heating large public buildings, including over five thousand churches. The Willington stove, a round, black cast iron structure with fins, surmounted with a crown or coronet, was originally sited in the north aisle near the north door so that it could be easily stoked with anthracite from a store-shed located nearby in the churchyard. These stoves proved both dirty and a fire-hazard and few have survived the coming of safer and more efficient forms of heating. (The Willington stove has now been re-sited in what might be felt by some to be an inappropriate and too prominent position on the north side of the chancel!)

Other minor, and some not so minor, improvements took place in the 1880s and 1890s. In 1884 a 1611 King James I Authorised Version of the Bible, then used at services in the Church, was restored by George Lambert, F.S.A., of London, at the instigation of Augustus. In 1885 the five-

7. King James I Authorised Version of the Bible of 1611.

light east window was filled with stained glass of the Ascension by Heaton, Butler and Bayne of Covent Garden, the Duke contributing another £200 towards the total cost of £320. In the same year and in 1886 other windows on the south side of the chancel and nave were supplied with glass which came from Southover in Sussex, Augustus's father-in-law's church, and another in Powell glass in his memory. In 1893 the embroidered panels on the reredos, worked by Caroline, were completed. The five bells, one of which had been cast in 1671 by Thomas Tompion, the great clockmaker originally from the neighbouring parish of Northill, were cracked and inharmonious and were recast and rehung in 1898. The work cost £225, for which the Duke gave £25. At the same time Augustus gave a sixth bell to mark his forty years of service to the parish.

In addition to all these improvements, in which Augustus, like all other parsons, took the lead, there was also the need to raise money within the parish to meet the day-to-day maintenance of the fabric of the church. For centuries these costs had been met by the levying of church rates on all property owners in the parish irrespective of their religious beliefs or none. Nonconformists, growing in numbers from the end of the 18th century, increasingly objected to these payments - determined in each parish by the churchwardens and the vestry meeting - which were levied for the upkeep of churches which they did not attend. The issue became a matter of vicious debate and dispute in the first half of the 19th century, until in 1868 compulsory church rates were abolished. The change brought relief to nonconformists but added considerably to pressure put on parishes to identify other sources of fund raising. This included income from pew rents which unfortunately reinforced exclusivity in those who considered themselves too good to worship in close proximity to their poorer neighbours. At Willington in 1896, whilst 153 seats were free, 30 were still rented.

Then, as now, it may have been easier to obtain financial support for specific projects than funding for general running expenses. Willington vestry accounts show that in many years the church was only kept out of the 'red' by a subvention from the Duke of Bedford: in 1878-9 a cheque of £15 from the Duke represented almost a third of total income whilst offertories were just short of a half in order to give a net credit balance on the year's operations of 13 shillings. Earlier, collections were only taken at Holy Communion with the money going to the poor, but later they were instituted at other services as well to meet general church expenses. Resort had to be made to what are still familiar church fund raising activities. Church fetes and bazaars were introduced although they were not universally favoured by all churchgoers as an appropriate means of meeting parochial expenses. Musical events, such as choral festivals and organ recitals, often under the auspices of the Church Music Society, were also held in the Church as a source of further income: in September 1875 Miss Havergal, daughter of the Rev. Henry Havergal of Cople, gave an organ recital in association with the annual harvest home. Some events were so adventurous that they involved the construction of temporary galleries in order to accommodate bigger 'audiences' and in April 1886, in association with one of these events, over 300 sat down to tea 'in the large barn', possibly the Tudor stables next to the Church. All these activities, whilst undoubtedly providing some income for the coffers of the church, were also important as epitomizing the church as the focal point of much of the social life of the village community. They helped also to reinforce the position of Augustus as the leader of that community.

Work as an Educationalist

Another activity in the village which greatly occupied Augustus's time and energy was the provision of education for children. It was primarily a secular activity although in the early days before the State took over it had significant religious overtones which have remained to a lesser extent to this day. Education for the poor children of the village certainly began with the Church. When Augustus arrived in the village in 1858 the only school in operation was a Sunday School located in a single storey building, still extant, on the corner opposite the east end of the Church at the junction of Church Road with Manor Road. (The building has long been a private house and much extended.) It had been built in 1832 at a cost of £132 on the initiative of the then non-resident vicar, the Rev. Dr. Philip Hunt, who was also Vicar of St. Peter's Church in Bedford. In its early days the school

8. Willington 'old' school building with upper storey addition;
building still extant but with further extensions.

appears to have had a chequered history: its financing was largely dependent upon subscriptions, attendance was irregular and the teachers unqualified. It at least kept poor village children occupied and out of mischief on the one day in the week when they were not working as well as giving a modicum of instruction in writing and spelling as preparation for reading the Bible. At the time of the Church School Inquiry of 1846/7 there were 41 Sunday scholars, 22 boys and 19 girls, who would go to classes from, perhaps, 9 – 10.45 a.m., before crossing the road to attend morning service - later under the eagle eye of Augustus - until possibly 12.30 p.m. or so.

No matter how well intentioned, all this was a very small step in the direction of universal popular education. Nevertheless, it is clear that the role of the local clergymen in its establishment and development was crucial. Augustus wished to widen and extend the educational opportunities open to the children of the poor in the village and to this end he promoted a day school in the Hunt building and engaged the services of a Miss Bromley from Cople to undertake the teaching. It was an uphill task since not all parents appreciated the value of education, especially when they were expected to pay for it and the attendance at school of even young children removed them from the pool of village labour and resulted in a drop in family earning power. Education was viewed by most parents as a nuisance which got in the way of children earning a livelihood. No one was too bothered about the use of child labour on farms until the 1860s and compulsory attendance at school had to await the provision of sufficient school places and legislation in the Education Act of 1880. Moreover, many members of the ruling classes believed that it might prove socially disruptive to educate the poor so that they aspired to live above the station in life into which they had been born. Tenant farmers saw education as being subordinate to agricultural production and in many instances thought more of the land than they did of those who worked it on their behalf. Fortunately, this was not a view to which Augustus subscribed. Over and above the importance which he assigned to education for the good and advancement of the poor, he also believed in the dignity of labour and the contribution it made to local and national well-being. Later in 1884 in a sermon given as Sheriff's Chaplain, Augustus demonstrates his feeling for the poor when preaching on the text 'Righteousness exalteth a nation'. He stated he saw it as the duty of the Church to improve the condition of the poor and to provide them with better homes. 'To the working class', he went on,' we owe the development of national greatness'.

The Church of England had already taken a lead in promoting the education of the poor by establishing in 1811 the National Society for Promoting the Education of the Poor in the Principles of the Established Church. After 1833 government money was made available, initially at the miniscule level of £20,000 a year, which the Society shared with its nonconformist counterpart, the British and Foreign Schools Society, for 'the erection of school houses' throughout the whole nation. This marked the beginning of a national system of public education. But for the continued generosity of the 9th Duke of Bedford, Willington would have had to wait a long time to bid into this limited funding in order to replace its existing totally inadequate day school.

In 1867 the Duke made available a sum of £1000 for the construction of a Church of England school under the aegis of the National Society. It opened on 31st August 1868 with the first pupils admitted personally by Augustus. He enrolled twelve children of whom only two could write their names, none had any idea of arithmetic and three screamed the whole morning after their mothers left them, wanting to go home. The building, of brick and tile construction, consisted of two

9. Willington 'new' school building of 1867.

classrooms, a large and a small one, the latter for the younger children and
the other for the older ones.   In addition, there were two enclosed yards to
the rear with storerooms and separate lavatories for boys and girls, the latter
reached on the east side by a covered way.   The Duke of Bedford believed
that children's minds were affected by the physical environment in which
they learned their lessons and, therefore, schoolrooms should offer healthy
conditions.   Little wonder that in a survey of all school buildings in the
County in 1904 at the time of the establishment of the Local Education
Authority, Willington School was one of only two schools which did not
require any form of repair or improvement.   The premises were referred to
as 'well lighted, lofty, airy and well warmed ...... excellent in build, and
upkeep.'   Certainly, in 1868 the building must have appeared state of the art

and that it is still in use to this day as the village school, albeit with modifications and extensions, is testimony to its design by Henry Clutton and the indefatigable efforts of Augustus to get the school built in the first place.

The new School provided for children of all ages. Attendance at the time being neither compulsory nor free, the age range was nevertheless from under five until generally twelve but occasionally thirteen or fourteen, although senior pupils were few in number because of the attraction of employment on the land for boys and lace-making and helping at home for girls. Attendance was poor and irregular. Reasons for absence given in the School logbook - required to be kept from 1863 - include haymaking, harvesting, carrying dinner to relatives working in the fields, lace-making, inadequate clothing and footwear during periods of severe weather, picking up acorns, gathering cowslips to make wine, watching the hunt and attending Chapel Sunday school treats. The overall roll of the School was generally between 40 and 50 when the total village population was 275 at the time of the 1871 census. In the return to the Education Department following the passage of the 1870 Education Act, it was calculated that the School could accommodate 130 pupils. There were, therefore, many families in the village who did not give their children the opportunity of attending school. Whilst it remained a church school, Augustus as vicar was very much in charge, soliciting subscriptions in order to finance its running, constantly visiting it, often in the company of his wife, and occasionally teaching, as well as encouraging attendance. Through the School, he was able to exert a strong influence on the thought and behaviour of the village as a whole. The young, and through them their parents, came to regard him with a certain awe and respect. He even made a family contribution to keeping up pupil numbers. His two daughters, Caroline and Margaret, attended the School for a time although they were let out of school to go home to the Vicarage at times different from other pupils.

All this must have represented an uphill task for Augustus and he must have faced the major change which took place in 1875 with the setting up of a school board with mixed feelings. In 1870 the State had taken a significant step forward in the provision of education for children of the poor. It was becoming increasingly clear that a voluntary system could not possibly educate the children of England. The Education Act of that year set out to provide a school place for every child. In areas where there were no schools, local school boards were established to build and run them. In addition, existing schools could be taken over and also run by the boards. Whilst this meant that the cost of running board schools would be met henceforth from public funds through grants from central government and the raising of rates locally, all board schools were also made subject to the direction and control of central government, including inspection by Her Majesty's Inspectors to ensure that educational standards were reached by pupils in order to earn financial support, i.e. a system of payment by results. Until 1891, when they were abolished, a smaller element of income was derived from fees on a sliding scale basis, usually one penny a week for the children of labourers and three pence from farmers and tradesmen with a reduced rate for more than one child in a family. Nevertheless, these changes, especially for church schools which became board schools, meant that such schools ceased to operate under the directing influence of local clergymen.

However, religious instruction remained an important factor in elementary education with Anglicans and Nonconformists jealously guarding their respective positions. As parents, under the 1870 Act, were given the right to withdraw their children from religious instruction, it was necessary for board schools to supply details of what they would provide. In 1878 the Willington Board determined that the Bible would be read and historically explained (Old and New Testaments on alternate mornings), from

9.10 to 9.45 a.m. each school day. No longer, as in a church school, could the parish priest decide such matters. Augustus found that, whilst financial worries were no more a major concern, he was no longer in the dominant position which he had previously enjoyed. He was henceforth, if elected, only one of five board members. He served, in fact, as a member for the whole life of the Willington Board from 1875 until 1903, although it was not until 1896 that he became Vice-Chairman and then Chairman from 1899. The remaining members were invariably tenant farmers who took a business approach to the running of the School and yet Augustus was the only member who had the time, experience and conviction to give to the job. It might very well have been that Augustus was seen by the other members as being too enthusiastic in his support of the education of the poor; certainly they were likely to be more concerned to keep down the rates and guarantee an ample supply of child labour for work on their farms. If curtailed in his activities in the school at Willington, Augustus nevertheless showed his willingness to support the establishment of schools elsewhere in the County. In December 1870 he contributed two guineas to an appeal launched by the local Church Board of Education for £1200 to bring provision in the County up to what it should be.

The new Willington School Board entered into an agreement with the Duke of Bedford, as the original provider of the school building, for its use as a public elementary day school at an annual rent of ten shillings. The Duke retained use of the building on Sundays, during school holidays and week day evenings. The Duke was also to keep the building, desks and fixtures in good repair and the School Board accepted responsibility for the rest, including all salaries and wages, rates, taxes and insurance premiums. However, the Duke continued to provide a wide ranging selection of educational materials and gifts to the School, including in 1883 maps, picture lessons, towels, bibles, a clock face, alphabet cards and animal pictures. It is clear that without the combination of the beneficence of the Duke of Bedford and the tenacity and enthusiasm for education of Augustus, the children of the village would not have received the opportunity for schooling as early as they did.

Like so many school boards elsewhere, the Willington Board operated, at least initially, under some difficulty. It was not always possible to obtain sufficient nominations for the election of the five managers: in fact, there was never a contested election throughout the life of the Board and, from time to time, members had to be co-opted. The School Board minute book shows that throughout the 1870s and 1880s many of the monthly meetings of the Board were inquorate. Pupils were not, therefore, set a good example by Board members of regular attendance. A former chairman was disqualified in 1880 by virtue of bankruptcy. The receipt of government grant was not only dependent on educational standards being reached by pupils but also regular attendance was required. Poor attendance resulted in a reduction in the amount of grant. The Board adopted bye-laws governing attendance of pupils and members of the Board were encouraged to visit the school and undertake spot checks on the attendance registers; Augustus was the most assiduous in doing this. Communications on the importance of regular attendance were sent to parents and employers in the village and legal proceedings were threatened against defaulting parents, although seldom instigated. Even prior to becoming Chairman of the Board, Augustus was deputed by his fellow members, no doubt because of his authority in the village, to take action on their behalf against the parents of truanting or 'mitching' children. In December 1877 Joshua Larkins was required to appear before him because of the poor attendance record of his daughter, Ellen. When he failed to appear, the father was prosecuted. It was very likely that other members of the Board as tenant farmers and employers were ambivalent in their attitude to attendance. (Acts of Parliament made attendance compulsory at school until the age of ten in 1880, eleven in 1893, twelve in 1899 and, eventually, fourteen in 1918, although exemptions permitted earlier leaving, providing certain standards of education had been attained and labour certificates permitting employment granted.)

10. Group of Willington school pupils c.1900, all spruced up for the photograph with the Headmistress, Emma Sandon, standing to the rear right.

Staffing of the School remained problematic until the arrival of Emma Sandon in 1889 and the beginning of her period of office of twenty-three years as Headmistress; before that between 1868 and 1879 there were six different headmistresses, probably because of poor pupil standards, parental opposition and pupil misbehaviour and ill-discipline. Miss Sandon brought stability and improved standards. As a means of keeping down expenditure, the Board did not engage the services of a second or assistant teacher and the employment of a pupil-teacher proved difficult and irregular; a monitor, paid only a few shillings a week and a former female pupil, not long herself out of the classroom, 'minded' rather than taught the youngest children under the supervision of the headmistress.

Even after it became a board school in 1875, Augustus continued in his former practice of frequently visiting the School.   In 1878 a complaint was made by the Headmistress that on one occasion he came to the School a few minutes after 12 o'clock and, after opening a private drawer in her desk, sat reading the School log book during the singing of Grace and the dismissal of pupils.   In the same year he interrupted a dictation lesson in order to invite any boy, to whom he would give six pence, to find a swarm of bees which he had lost.   Again in 1880 another Headmistress complained to the Board of the way she had been addressed by Augustus at the previous meeting and the remarks he had made about her proficiency as a teacher. There are no more details of these incidents: in defence of Augustus's actions, both of these head-teachers served at the School for only short periods and Augustus, because of his experience and commitment to the importance of education, was likely to speak out against any professional shortcomings which he observed in the School.   Other managers were unlikely to be able to make such judgments even if they took their responsibilities seriously.   Nevertheless, it is clear that Augustus still viewed the School as part of his domain.

Clearly, after the mammoth change in arrangements after 1875, Augustus, committed as he was to the education of the poor, did not find it easy to adjust to a less dominant role in relation to the running of the village school.   Nevertheless, as time progressed, and the value and importance of education became more widely acknowledged, standards of attainment gradually improved and attendance became more regular, Augustus was able to adopt a more relaxed attitude to what went on in the School.   In 1895 when, as part of the annual School Treat, senior pupils produced a village alphabet, it included:

> *O is for Orlebar, our Vicar for Years.*
> *Before he leaves here we will give him three cheers.*

Even as late as 1905 when over 80, Augustus had not given up the educational battle: he took an active part in resisting an attempt by the LEA to close the school in the village and combine it in a new school building in Cople.   Such a move would have put at risk an important part of village life and, even then, it was considered too far for young children to walk to and from school.   It is highly probable that Augustus would have made representations direct to the Duke of Bedford, by then Herbrand the 11th Duke, who, as it so happened, was Chairman of the County Council.

Other Work in the Parish and Beyond

In addition to encouraging and promoting activities in the village, Augustus was also active in the support of organisations and interests in the immediate neighbourhood and throughout the County and beyond. As a cleric it was only natural that a great deal of his time and energies should be taken up with church matters both in and around Bedford and on a wider front at diocesan level. In 1866 the first diocesan conference met at Ely and in the early 1870s Augustus at first assisted the Diocesan Secretary and then for a time was Diocesan Organising Secretary, 'discharging his duties with zeal and energy' and involving lengthy and tortuous rail journeys to Ely and elsewhere. (Whilst the Bedford-Cambridge line ran through the parish from 1862, cutting through the glebe land, a station for passenger traffic was not opened until 1903. This would have meant that for the bulk of his time as vicar, Augustus would have had to travel by 'horsepower' to the railhead at Sandy Junction for an onward journey to Cambridge and Ely either directly to Cambridge or via Hitchin, involving perhaps an overnight stay away from the village.)

His early days as a poorly paid curate, and then vicar of a parish with a small income, made him a strong supporter of bodies to assist clergymen with small livings and low stipends. In 1875 he seconded a resolution at the Bedford Archidiaconal Conference for the establishment of a diocesan fund to augment the income from small livings, of which at the time a half were at the level of £300 a year or less. From 1877 he was Hon. Secretary of the Beds. Society for the Relief of Necessitous Clergy and, between 1874 and the time of his death, Organising Secretary of the Diocesan Branch of the Additional Curates Society founded in 1837. From 1868 until 1910 he was Secretary of the Biggleswade Clerical Association which demonstrates his awareness of the need to help develop a corporate identity amongst the clergy as its role in society became more professional. Acting in a pastoral capacity to his fellow clergy in the neighbourhood, he was Rural Dean of Haynes from 1874 to 1911, until his health began to fail. These many honorary posts, held over long periods of time, show that he had good organising and administrative abilities and had the trust and confidence of his fellow clergy. These skills would undoubtedly have equipped him for advancement within the Church and he could have done well working at diocesan level. He was a frequent preacher in neighbouring parishes and further afield and at various times he served as Sheriff's Chaplain. Although not himself teetotal, he was a member of the local committee of the Church of England Temperance Society, recognising the social evils of drink and speaking against its excesses. He also encouraged a local branch of the Band of Hope for children which were to be found in most places of nonconformist worship and which urged the signing of a pledge to abstain from alcohol. Augustus was, however, a non-smoker. In 1896 he became chairman when a village club was formed for social purposes, again, in the absence of a village hall, making use of the old schoolroom.

In secular matters in the neighbourhood, Augustus was equally active. He came from a family which traditionally was Tory in its support when it came to national politics. Before the passage of the Secret Ballot Act of 1872, it is possible to ascertain how the small number of electors voted by reference to the printed poll books which recorded open voting on the hustings. At the time of the 1857 General Election, he cast his vote in the two member County constituency for the Whig candidates Hastings Russell and William Higgins of Turvey, although the latter was not returned. This may have been against Augustus's natural Tory inclinations, but perhaps nevertheless a judicious move on his part when he was seeking advancement in the church. It might be said to have paid off when the next year he was appointed by the Duke of Bedford, a Whig magnate, to the living of Willington. However, by the time of the last open election in

1872 - a by-election resulting from the death of the 8th Duke of Bedford and Hastings Russell succeeding him as 9th Duke - Augustus had switched his party allegiance and voted for the Tory candidate, William Stuart of Tempsford, an acknowledged 'church' candidate. (At the time, Augustus was one of only six males in the parish eligible to vote by virtue of the property they held. Between 1857 and 1872 some elections were uncontested and for others poll books are missing. It was not until the Franchise Act of 1884 that agricultural labourers were given the vote and the electorate widened but still did not include women.)

At a local level in public affairs, Augustus was for many years a member of the Management Committee of Bedford County Hospital as well as a Poor Law Guardian for the Parish. When the Parish Council was first set up in 1906, Augustus became a member, although generally the establishment of parish councils had the effect of reducing the authority of the squire and the parson. (Parish councils had been set up under the Local Government Act of 1894 but parishes with a population of less than 300 had to be content with an annual parish meeting instead of a council.) By virtue of their family backgrounds, Augustus and Caroline had automatic entrée into the upper echelons of Bedfordshire society, particularly in the east and north of the County - the Polhill-Turners at Howbury Hall, the Thorntons at St. John's, Moggerhanger, the Barnards at Cople, the Burgoynes at Sutton Park. (Their youngest son, Edward, who entered the Church and became Vicar of Steeple Morden, married a Thornton.) They had an extensive circle of friends and were in frequent attendance at a wide range of social gatherings; their names are seldom missing from the press listings of those attending weddings, as invited present-giving guests, and funerals. In July 1880 they were among those present at Woburn Abbey on the occasion of a day visit by the Prince and Princess of Wales, later Edward VII and Queen Alexandra.

With an interest in agriculture as a result of working the glebe and other parcels of land in the village, Augustus was a staunch supporter of the Beds. Agricultural Show. In 1882 he took first prize for a 1lb. of red currants at the Sandy Show, and probably much else on other occasions both there and elsewhere. It was acknowledged that he kept the finest herd of Alderney cattle in the area. Augustus took an active lead in the organisation of village harvest home suppers to celebrate the completion of the gathering in of the annual harvest, holding them on many occasions in the grounds of the Vicarage with prizes for flowers and vegetables.

Throughout his lifetime, Augustus maintained an interest and participation in a wide range of sporting activities. Walking and horse riding were constant pursuits in which he engaged. In the Vicarage he had a portrait of his godfather, William Augustus, in hunting attire on a favourite hunter. There is no evidence, however, that Augustus, whilst a horseman, rode to hounds. He was a good swimmer. From 1875 he was a member of the Bedford Croquet Club, gaining his last prize at the age of 84 in 1908. As the years progressed, his previous interest in cricket passed to tennis, although he continued to promote and encourage a village cricket team which held its own against teams from larger villages: in 1887 it beat a team from Potton by four runs and, when at home from school or university, Augustus's sons took part. He also encouraged, and probably coached, his daughter, Caroline, who was captain of a ladies team and considered 'a demon bowler'. From the 1870s Augustus was a member of the County Lawn Tennis Club, taking part in tournaments although seldom progressing beyond the first round – perhaps as a result of pairings with untalented partners! In his later years Augustus spent his evenings playing bridge and his mornings keeping his mind alert by reading a Greek testament. He was a great dog lover.

Improving the Lives of Villagers

Prior to Augustus's arrival in 1858, Balls Lane was little more than 'a common country grass lane' – much as Jake's Drive is today – but important in allowing carts to gain access to the Bedford-Sandy road from the western end of the village.   Augustus was instrumental in having it straightened and providing the first loads of gravel to improve its surface.   As an antiquarian, he was extremely proud of the Church as a building and the remains of the Manor and the stables and dovecote – the latter two not then in the ownership of the National Trust - and was keen to show them to visitors.

11. Village transport c.1905 with children outside the Vicarage in Church Road, Willington.

He made a study of the Gostwick family history, including the construction of a family tree, and supported the meetings and excursions of the Bedford Archaeological and Architectural Society.   Augustus acted as the enumerator for the parish of the censuses every decade, completing in his own hand the returns, and was much in demand for providing references for young boys or girls seeking jobs or signing legal documents as a person of education and standing.

In the early 1870s when there was trouble in the area over the level of agricultural wages, Augustus did not act as did his near neighbour, the Rev. Henry Havergal of Cople, in giving active support to the labourers' cause against their farmer employers. Throughout the middle decades of the 19th century at a time of good harvests, aided by land drainage schemes, British farmers prospered. However, farm labourers did not share in this prosperity; they remained generally in abject poverty, poorly paid, ill-housed, miserably fed, scantily clothed, voteless and uneducated; their life was one of unremitting toil. Usual hours of work on the land were 6 a.m. to 6 p.m. in summer and 7 a.m. till dark in winter. Resentment had also been aroused from labourers by the passage of the Poaching Prevention Act of 1862. It introduced what in effect was a 'stop and search policy' since any villager could be apprehended if carrying a bundle after working hours. Agricultural labourers were in effect in economic and political serfdom. In these circumstances, it was not unnatural that labourers wanted more pay and shorter hours of work. In the Spring of 1874 when agricultural labourers refused to work at the current rate of pay of 13 shillings a week during the winter months, Havergal supported and encouraged them to join Joseph Arch's National Agricultural Labourers' Union (NALU), which was strong in the Midlands and the Eastern Counties. Membership of the Union rapidly expanded, members paying an entry fee of 6d. and thereafter 2d. a week. When many farmers retaliated by threatening eviction from their farm-tied cottages of those who joined the Union and locked-out the labourers from working for eighteen weeks, there was general unrest and hardship in the area. The Union's aim was a pay rate of 16 shillings a week and a nine and half hour day. Many saw emigration as a palliative to over-population and poverty and a number of Cople labourers and their families are recorded as emigrating in 1874. The irony in Arch's 'Grace' succinctly summarises the labourers' condition:

> *O Heavenly Father bless us*
> *And keep us all alive;*
> *There are ten of us at table*
> *And food for only five.*

Havergal became Secretary of the Cople Branch of the NALU where some 60 labourers were locked-out. He opened the schoolroom daily as a reading and recreation room, wrote an open letter to the Duke of Bedford in March 1874, referring to aggrieved cottagers in both Cople and Willington, and in early July 1874 headed a march, together with the General Secretary of the NALU, through the streets of Bedford to a

12. Estate cottages in Church Road, Willington,
the centre block (Nos. 44-50) demolished in the 1960s.

gathering of over one thousand protesting labourers on the Market-hill, near St. Paul's Church. Havergal's actions in interfering with 'the management of property' were attacked in the correspondence columns of the *Bedfordshire Times and Independent* as being 'mischievous and perilous' and an incitement of an insurrection of labour against capital. Also, Havergal spoke out against the farmers from the pulpit and thereby demonstrated active support for the labourers; his attitude was exceptional in a clergyman.

We know very little of the extent to which Willington labourers were affected by the unrest. Certainly, for many their accommodation was generally much better than elsewhere if living in the brick and slate estate cottages provided by the dukes of Bedford in 1849 and 1857-8, and later in 1890, with the opportunity also to rent additional land for cultivation. (Most of these cottages still remain on the north side of Church Road, with a stone plaque in their gables bearing a coronet, a 'B' – for Bedford - and the date of their construction, as does the School also.) The allotments, usually of 20 poles each and rented at 2d to 4d per pole in 1867, constituted an important fringe benefit for agricultural labourers, providing a cheap and improved family diet. There was the strict proviso that the allotments could not be worked after 6 a.m. or before 6 p.m. on working days, without the permission of employers. In addition, all occupiers were expected 'to conduct themselves with propriety at all times, and to bring up their families in a decent and orderly manner' – something which Augustus would also have expected.

Press comments indicate that some Willington farmers participated in the lock-out. What we do know is that, unlike Havergal, there is no indication that Augustus did anything to become actively involved in the dispute. It is likely that he would have sought to placate and mediate rather than openly take sides and thereby fuel the confrontation. As a member of a local landed family and with the Duke of Bedford owning practically all the cottages in the village, he was likely to have been sympathetic to the position of the Duke's agent and the tenant farmers, whilst at the same time seeking to aid and support those villagers adversely affected in their everyday lives by the unrest. Being a leading clergyman in the area, had he followed Havergal's stance he would certainly have drawn attention to himself and it would have been recorded at the time, as with Havergal, for us to know about. Like Willington, Cople was part of the Bedfordshire Russell estates and the agricultural labourers of both parishes would have enjoyed the beneficial treatment at the hands of their common landlord, the Duke of Bedford. It may have been, of course, that the tenant farmers of Cople took a harder line with their labourers than did their counterparts in Willington; conversely, Willington labourers may have been either more contented or lethargic – or did Augustus have a firmer grip on things?

What, however, the differing attitudes of Augustus and Havergal on the issue would seem to indicate is the strong influence which local clergy, whatever their views, had over the lives and destinies of the labouring poor of their parishes. Both Augustus and Havergal wished to see an improvement in the lot of the poor, but Augustus, like the majority of clergymen, did not seek its achievement by encouraging activities and movements which might inadvertently undermine and disrupt an otherwise stable and ordered society. (After 18 weeks of lock-out and the advent of the harvest, there was a gradual return to 'normality' in the closing months of 1874: some labourers had migrated or emigrated and others returned to work with a reduction in wages, in some parts of the district by 1s. to 2s. a week; there was disenchantment with the Union, which by July 1875 had split into two sections when claims of discrepancies in its accounts were

13. Haymaking in the Village early 1900s.

revealed; trade unionism in agriculture had received a serious setback and labour relations had been tarnished; in January 1875 Havergal died of apoplexy after 27 years as Vicar of Cople and labourers of the parish raised £3 17s towards a tombstone.)

A widespread agricultural depression in the last quarter of the 19th century, due to unseasonable weather, outbreaks of disease amongst livestock and an overwhelming increase in overseas competition from the importing of cheap foreign-grown grain and refrigerated meat, had an immense impact on British farming and the economy of the countryside; landlords and farmers were hit as well as labourers.   The year 1879 was the worst, with a summer which lacked sunshine and greater rainfall that usual and resulting in a failure of the harvest; pleura-pneumonia and foot-and-mouth were rampant among cattle and three million sheep were lost by rot. The nadir was not reached until 1895, although thereafter things began to pick up. Willington, like elsewhere in East Bedfordshire, was in a better position than other parts of the country to come through this period of rural depression. Cattle grazing, sheep rearing and arable farming with wheat, barley, peas and beans the main crops, whilst not entirely abandoned, were gradually replaced by a shift to market gardening. In addition to suitable soil conditions, it was the presence of a developing rail network which was crucial to the increased growth of market gardening: fresh perishable commodities could be transported speedily to large centres of population such as London and the West Midlands and supplies of horse manure could be brought back to improve productivity still further. By 1910 Kelly's Directory listed five market gardeners and one nurseryman and a florist in the village.

The depression also had other effects: a decline in the price of grain and livestock resulted in a drop in the rents of agricultural land and a displacement of labour. The Duke of Bedford was forced not only to remit rents in general but also to sell off his large Thorney and Tavistock estates in Cambridgeshire and Devon respectively as well as the much smaller one of

14. Dairyman's cart and farmworkers in the Village early 1900s.

Willington in 1902. At that time Augustus took the opportunity to add to his own property holding in the village. At the third sale in Sandy in 1903 he bought eight acres of pasture for £460 and three stud and thatched cottages with a little land for £280. When prices had risen, wages had dropped and, with the introduction of more machinery, many labourers lost their jobs. There was an inevitable drift to the towns in search of alternative employment. The census returns for the parish show a fall in 1881 from 248 inhabitants to 234 in 1891 and 204 in 1901, rising again by 1911 to 370 with more house building taking place along Bedford Road and Chapel Lane. It was Augustus, as the head of the village community, who was expected to provide aid and succour during this difficult period for parishioners; in 1891, when there was a particularly poor harvest, he and Caroline set up a temporary soup kitchen for the benefit of villagers. All this must have placed heavy demands upon his sense of pastoral care and mission. The endless round of cottage visiting, not only to the chronic sick and bedridden but also those temporarily in need, became all the more important, as did the more regular gifts and handouts of beef, broth and milk. But for the provision by the dukes of Bedford of land to cottagers, it is likely that Augustus would have busied himself with the provision of allotments which many country clergy promoted as a means of alleviating agricultural hardship. Moreover, the later predominance of market gardening in the village, giving access to cheap fruit and vegetables, made less likely malnutrition and the worst effects of poverty.

'The Father of the Village'

An incident in 1882 when nearing the age of sixty demonstrates Augustus's fitness in body and his concern for others to the point of self-sacrifice. On a summer evening in that year, a group of seven or eight village lads, including Herbert Balls, a fifteen year old and a member of the church choir, decided about 8 p.m. to take a dip in the river. Balls was a non-swimmer and got into difficulties in a deep hole. On hearing of the occurrence, Augustus, accompanied by his son Evelyn, got his boat to where Balls had been last seen and dived several times into the water. He was unable immediately to locate and recover the body but eventually, with the use of oars, was able to drag the body to the south bank of the river where, by then, Caroline was waiting with blankets, brandy and hot water to try and revive the boy. Unfortunately, this was in vain and at an inquest later, held in the old schoolroom, a verdict of accidental death by drowning was recorded. Although unsuccessful in his efforts to save the boy, Augustus was nevertheless feted as a local hero.

At various landmarks in his personal life and that of his family, the villagers joined in celebrations and used such occasions as a means of demonstrating the high regard and esteem in which they held Augustus and his family. When in 1884 Augustus and Caroline celebrated their silver wedding, the parishioners presented them with a drawing-room clock, candlesticks and a bell of antique brass. In 1889 when their second son, George, went out to India to commence working as a bailiff on a coffee plantation, the villagers gave him a gold pencil. When in 1893 their second son, Evelyn, a lieutenant in the Royal Marines, was married at the fashionable church of St. James's, Piccadilly, in London, with Augustus officiating, the parishioners gave the married couple a picture clock. To celebrate the occasion, Augustus and Caroline in return gave the parishioners 'a substantial repast' spread in the schoolroom followed by entertainment by a ventriloquist and conjurer, Professor Du Cann of

Northampton.   In 1894 the Orlebars gave the village a tea to mark the marriage of the Duke of York and Princess May, later George V and Queen Mary; once again the grounds of the vicarage were pressed into service.

The whole village was thrown into mourning on Caroline's death early in 1904 at the age of seventy-six after a brief illness of only five days.

15. Caroline Orlebar in later life.

She had been a tremendous helpmate to her husband, acting as choirmaster and playing first the harmonium, and then the organ, in the Church for over forty years, as well as plying her needle to decorate altar frontals and screens and helping in the School.   The local press recorded that 'her bright and kindly visits to the homes of parishioners of Willington were a frequent source of help and encouragement'. She was buried in the north side of the churchyard with snowdrops in greenery of moss and ivy arranged on the grave by the vicarage gardener, Sam Scotton, and William Spavins.

A far happier village celebration later that year in July was the marking of Augustus's fifty years of service to the parish. Church Road was bedecked with flags and pennants and the location of the celebrations was the lawn of the Vicarage. In one part of the garden a wide canvas awning shaded several long tea-tables and a splendid repast had been prepared by the vicarage household, assisted by neighbours. The guests were mainly drawn from the village but members of Augustus's family were also present. Before partaking of the 'feast', the company was entertained by Funny Scrubbs and games and amusements were provided on the lawn and in the adjoining field. At the close of the tea, Augustus was given the opportunity to address the assembled company. He said he was thankful to God that he was able to entertain so many of his parishioners after fifty years of great happiness in the parish and he thanked them for the kindness he had received over the years. He referred to the fact that twice he had received invitations to important livings elsewhere but that both he and his wife had felt that it was unlikely that they would be as happy as in Willington. He then reminisced on the changes which had taken place in the village since he first arrived. He was particularly pleased to note the increase in wages and improvements in the standard of living of villagers. When he came an able-bodied man earned no more than nine shillings a week; wages were then much higher and they had better cottages and land provided by the dukes of Bedford. He wished to thank the villagers for their support over so many years and for the pleasure and happiness they had given him and his family. As a small token of his appreciation he wished to present to the parish new ropes for the Church bells. He sat down to loud applause.

*16. North (rear) view of the Vicarage before the demolition
of this wing in the late 1960s.*

It was then the turn of the parishioners. William Harris of Croot's
Farm spoke on their behalf and, after paying tribute to Augustus, he asked
him to accept a silver rose bowl, embossed and chased in a design of roses
and foliage and mounted on an ebony pedestal, to which villagers had
subscribed freely and cheerfully, together with an album, bound in
Morocco leather and artistically illuminated, containing an address which
expressed the feelings of every parishioner – applause. Others also spoke
in support, including Isaac Godber as a newcomer to the village. Augustus
was clearly overcome and briefly thanked the villagers for their gift. He
was pleased to know that everyone in the village had such good will
towards him. Augustus's eldest son, Augustus, also responded on behalf of
the family, after which the gifts were inspected. Thereafter, the old folk

talked, the young, including 'village maidens', played cricket, the middle-aged bowls and young men tried their skill at the national game of football in the meadow beyond.   Could there be a more idyllic and pleasing scene?

Augustus had only four more years left to him but he had every intention of seeing out his days as Vicar of his beloved Willington.   (If he retired there was no pension since a full modern scheme for clergymen was not introduced by the Church of England until the 1920s.)   A birthday notice which appeared in the local press in June 1911 spoke of his 'excellent health, upright bearing, manly voice, quickness of perception and firm step of a man half his age'.   However, in October of that year, during a holiday at Brighton, he contracted a chill, which today would

17. The Reverend Augustus Orlebar in later life.

likely be diagnosed as a virus, and which developed into bronchitis. Early in 1912 he suffered a slight stroke and outside the vicarage was confined to a wheelchair. He was then assisted in his priestly duties by his schoolfellow, the Rev. J.P. Langley, formerly Vicar of Olney and in retirement resident in Bedford, until it became necessary to appoint a curate, the Rev. Wanborough Jones. By the end of September 1912, it was clear that the end was near and the family were summoned. Augustus died on 30th September 1912, death being due to bronchitis and 'senile decay'.

The funeral took place on Thursday 3rd October. It was a sunny but cold day. A large congregation of family and friends filled the Church. There were present a large number of neighbouring clergy, including the Bishop of Ely. The service was choral with the choir of St. Paul's, Bedford, in attendance. In addition to family flowers, a wreath from villagers was hung over the lectern and attached to the pulpit was another bearing the words: 'In loving memory of our dear Vicar, from Miss Sandon and children of Willington School.' He was laid to rest in the churchyard beside his wife, Caroline, and later a memorial tablet, by A. Wrighton of Bedford, was placed on the north wall of the chancel of the Church. In 1914 new oak choir desks, by Gill of St. Neots, were installed also in memory of Augustus and his elder daughter, Caroline, who died in 1913.

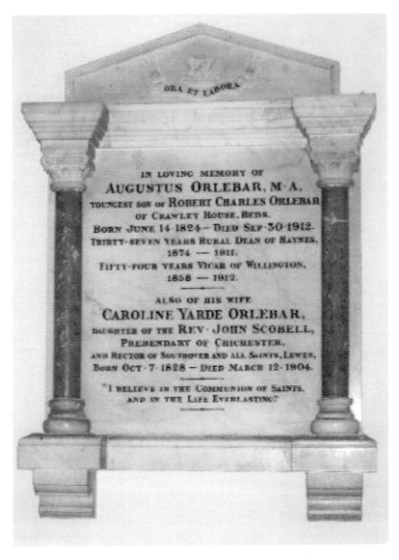

18. *Memorial tablet to Augustus and Caroline on the*
north wall of the chancel in Willington Church

Epitaph

It was wholly appropriate that the children of the village should have paid tribute to Augustus in the way they did. Second only to his dedication to his priestly tasks and duties were his efforts to widen opportunities for the education of the children of the village. A hundred years on, the restored village church and the school are living physical reminders of what he achieved for the community. His vicarage, now a private dwelling, remains in Church Road in the heart of the village as a symbol of the central position which it and its occupant held in the lives of villagers throughout his time as parish priest. Whilst Augustus's interests and activities went beyond the confines of the village, it was primarily as parish priest and, in the absence of a resident landlord and squire, as head of the village community that his influence was paramount; it was a role he fulfilled naturally and with ease by virtue of his background, upbringing and education. He brought a civilising influence to the village. He was that most attractive of personalities - an all-round man of broad interests, as well as being caring, business-like, methodical and painstaking. The report on his death in the *Bedfordshire Times and Independent* of 4th October 1912 referred to him as 'a man of most genial and courteous presence' and ' one of the most remarkable personalities in the County'. Above all, he found satisfaction and contentment in ministering to the spiritual and welfare needs of his 'flock'. Being without ecclesiastical ambition, he shunned further promotion within the Church, refusing preferment on a number of occasions. His daily work in the parish - admittedly enlivened by diverse interests beyond its boundaries - was for him its own reward and the fact that he, and the villagers, survived together for over fifty years is testimony enough to the mutual trust and respect which sustained that relationship. He had an abiding regard for the parish and that was reciprocated by the villagers. In such circumstances, the sobriquet 'Father of the Village' was earned with full justification. As a parish tribute at the time recorded: 'Everyone in the Parish grieved at the death of Mr Orlebar.   His great abilities and complete devotion to the good of his fellows endeared him to a wide circle of friends; we, as near neighbours, loved him for his kindness of heart, genial manners and readiness to help in every good cause'.

'His works do follow him'

Bibliography

Addison, William, The English Country Parson, 1977

Bedfordshire County Council, Guide to the Russell Estate Collections, 1966

Bedfordshire Historical Record Society:

      Vol. 60   (Agar, Nigel E.) The Bedfordshire Farm Worker in the
                    Nineteenth Century, 1981

      Vol. 67   (Bushby, David) The Bedfordshire Schoolchild, 1988

      Vol. 79   (Pickford, Chris) Bedfordshire Churches in the
                    Nineteenth Century, Part III Parishes S to Y, 2000

      A Bedfordshire Bibliography (Conisbee, L.R. Threadgill, A.R.)
                    4 Vols., 1962-78

Bell, Patricia, Belief in Bedfordshire, 1986

Chadwick, Owen, The Victorian Church, 1970

Clark, G. Kitson, Churchmen and the Condition of England 1832-85, 1973

Colloms, Brenda, Victorian Country Parsons, 1977

Cruickshank, M., Church and State in English Education:
                    1870 to the Present Day, 1963

Curtis, S.J., History of Education in Great Britain, (Seventh Edition) 1967

Ernle, Lord, English Farming, Past and Present, (Sixth Edition) 1961

Fawthrop, Audrey, Willington Lower School, 1986

Godber, Joyce   The History of Bedfordshire, 1965
                    Willington (Pamphlet), n.d. [c.1970]

Green, F.E., A History of the English Agricultural Labourer 1870-1921, 1920

Hart, A. Tindall, and Carpenter, Edward, The Nineteenth Century Country
                    Parson, 1954

Horn, Pamela, Labouring Life in the Victorian Countryside, 1976

Houfe, Simon, Bedfordshire, 1995

Hughes, Thomas, Tom Brown's Schooldays, 1867

Huitson, Jennifer, The Parish Church of St. Lawrence, Willington, n.d. [c.1985]

Martin , E.W., The Secret People, English Village Life after 1750, 1954

May, Trevor, The Victorian Clergyman, 2006

Trent, Christopher, The Russells, 1966

Victoria County History, Bedfordshire (Part 29, Wixamtree Hundred), 1912

Vowles, Gordon, A Century of Achievement, A History of L.E.A.s
                in Bedfordshire, 2003

Willington Women's Institute, Scrapbook, 1955